Art by Cliff Richards, Julio Ferreira, and Jeromy Cox

Buffy THE VAMPIRE SLAYER™

GOT NO IDEA, ANGEL. NO IDEA AT ALL.

HAUNTED

based on the television series created by
JOSS WHEDON

writer **JANE ESPENSON**

penciller **CLIFF RICHARDS**

inker **JULIO FERREIRA**

colorist **JEROMY COX**

letterer **CLEM ROBINS**

This story takes place after Buffy the Vampire Slayer's third season.

Titan books

TWO YEARS EARLIER.

Campfires. Gotta love 'em! Gosh, don't they bring back all **kinds** of good memories?

Away from home for the first time. Maybe you're wearing a little uniform--Boy Scouts or Girl Scouts or, Lord love 'em, the Campfire Girls...

And there you are, under the stars, gathered 'round that ol' campfire, your eyes wide and glowing...

Maybe someone starts telling ghost stories...

In fact, I think I'll tell one myself. Not traditionally the job of a **mayor**, but then I was never a traditional mayor.

SKKSH

Would you like to hear a joke? Here it is. I just flew in from the flaming remains of the high school and boy are my arms tired.

The broken wings of my borrowed body aches. I'm surprised to find that I feel the pain. I won't be able to fly again. I need to get out of this body...

My revulsion is leaving me. All I can think about is my goal. My REVENGE.

...And into something new.

I need a new body. Nothing fancy, just good basic transportation.

A body that can take me to the Slayer.

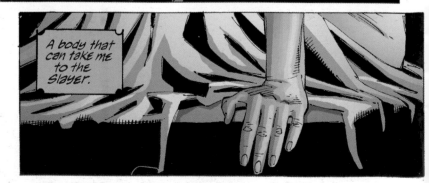

KA-WHOMP

Once free, I swim through the earth. It's as easy as moving through air or water. Delightful.

I look around...

...do some window shopping...

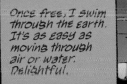

GRRRAAGH

ARRRRK

...until I find something just right.

No revulsion now. I feel only eagerness and anticipation. This is fun!

GRRRGHHH

GRRRRRK?

Both the dead bodies I had occupied up to this point had been empty. This one is not. But dead is dead. I move in.

There is a mind in here, but there is no soul. It's easy to kick it out. I am a ghost with a purpose, and that gives me strength.

If I'd known this kind of activity could be so exhilarating I would have participated more in athletics when I was alive.

TOK

BAM

It was a fine body. It's broken now. I suppose I could force it to keep going, but I have a growing intellectual curiosity about something.

SHNNNK

STAKE

It is a unique sensation.

This bird is lower quality than the last one.

I can feel the maggots moving around inside it. But that kind of thing bothers me less and less. Gosh, it's liberating to leave a phobia behind.

How are you, Sweetheart? I hope there are *circuses* and *delights* inside your head.

I have things to tell you, Sweetheart. For example, did you know I was just in a vampire?

It was the most amazing feeling. And when the body turned to dust, I wasn't sad. I was **galvanized**, because I realized something...

...I realized that I could do it *over* and *over* and *over* again. I can terrorize the Slayer and her friends with a torment that never ends, just like yours. And she'll never even realize it's all one spirit against her.

She'll never know it's me.

I'M OFF MY GAME. *WAY OFF.* I CAN'T EVEN *SEE* THE GAME FROM HERE. I DON'T KNOW IF IT HAS TO DO WITH THE DREAMS OR NOT...I SCREAMED EARLIER TONIGHT WHEN I SAW THAT FIRST VAMP. THEN I LET GILES GET HURT--

BUFFY, YOU DID NOT *"LET"*--

NO, IT'S TRUE. I'M *EXHAUSTED.* IT'S LIKE, I GAVE UP EVERYTHING I HAD FOR THAT FIGHT ON GRADUATION DAY, AND NOW ...NOW I HAVE TO FIND MORE, AND MAYBE IT'S JUST NOT THERE.

BUFFY, *SHHH.* IT'S OKAY. YOU'RE NOT ALONE, YOU KNOW? WE'LL TAKE GILES HOME, GATHER EVERYONE TOGETHER FIRST THING IN THE MORNING...WE CAN DO THIS, EVEN IF GILES CAN'T HELP. LET *US* HELP. TELL US WHAT TO DO AND WE'LL HELP.

Gosh, it's interesting. It no longer disgusts me to occupy the body of a vampire. I mean, I guess it's odd not to look like myself.

But the coldness of the flesh wrapped around my wandering soul feels comforting and *right*, and, kinda...neat.

I like the way the sinews in this new body--well, new to me, *ha ha*--already partially dissolved by the process of decay, have been hardened, **strengthened**, made better than they were in life.

The eyes see in the dark. Even now, before the moon rises, I can see every little detail.

Very handy.

WE'RE CUTTING IT CLOSE. THE MOON'S ABOUT TO RISE.

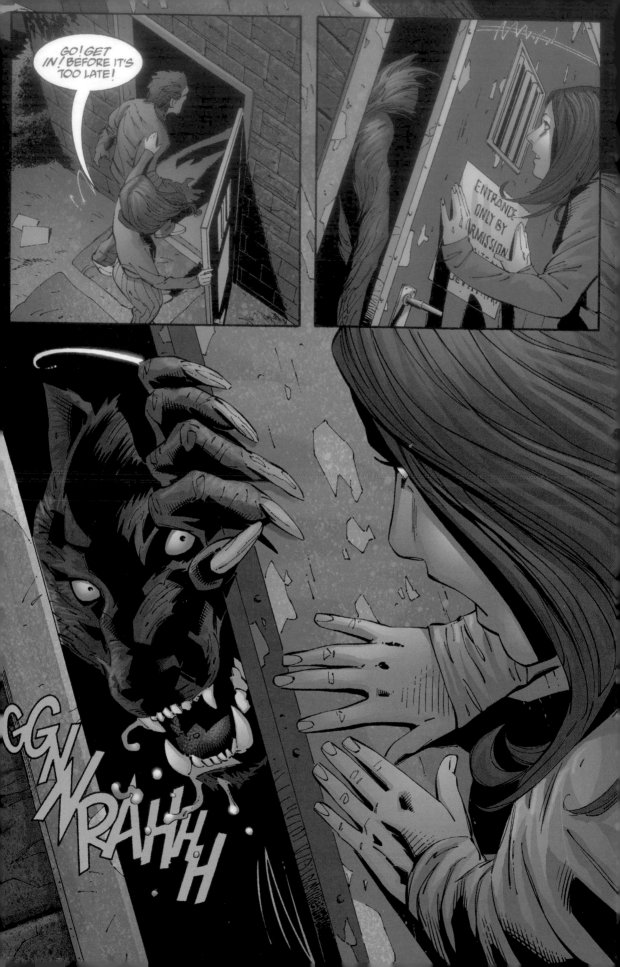

I am seized by an odd compulsion. Or maybe... maybe it isn't that odd after all. Maybe it's natural.

KRAAAK

It is like drinking life itself.

And I begin to wonder who is possessing whom. But, then again, as long as I keep my goal in mind...

...I don't really care.

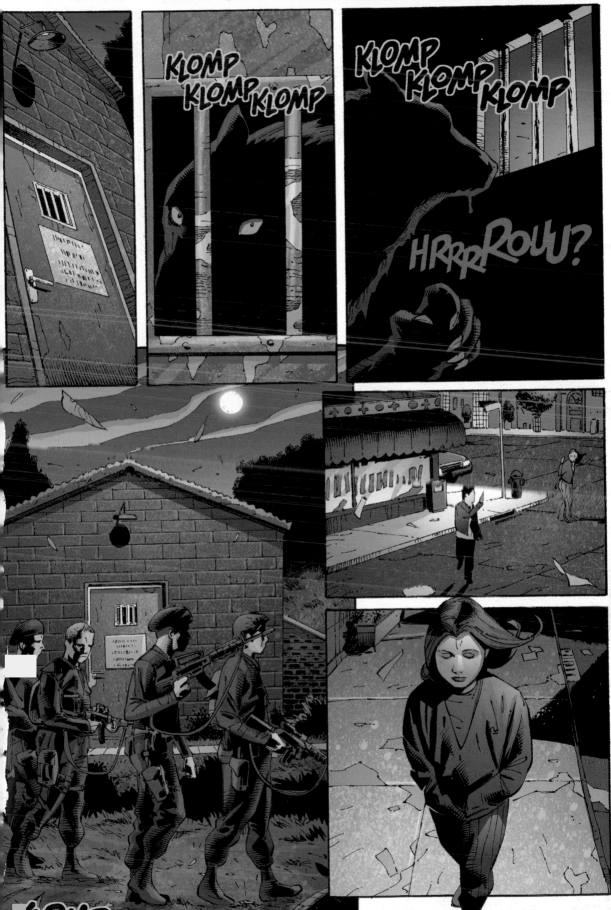

Oops. Dropped something.